DILIGENT PURSUIT OF

Well Done

KAREN WEHUNT HARDEN

1

Independently Published

Amazon/ Kindle

ISBN: 9798864708545

Karen Harden

wharden1950@gmail.com

All scriptures are from the KJV

Cover by David Hortta

Author photo by Kate Wiggins

Holt Publishing (holtpublishing4U@gmail.com)

Dedication

To my best friend and husband,

Jim Harden,

who has seen me through

thick-and-thin for thirty-eight years.

Table of Contents

Katio is our Patio for the Cats.

Acknowledgements

Friends and neighbors who gave me technological assistance and encouragement.

Vickie Hodge Holt – Mentor and Publisher

David Hortta – Cover Designer and Illustrator

Miss Kate Wiggins – Author's Photo

Bunny Bishop – *Speak for Animals*

Introduction
A Sense of Urgency

At almost seventy-three years old,

I need to hurry up and say what needs to be said before:

I die,

Forget what I meant to say,

And/or

Run out of steam.

Plan A: I look forward to hearing, "Well done, good and faithful servant, come and take thy rest."

Plan B: To be met by the Welcoming Committee.

Plan C: The Gate will be opened; for all my life, you have been faithful to me.

The overarching theme of this collection is to be an encouragement by imparting the wisdom gleaned from others over a lifetime in the diligent pursuit of well done. Remember:

Trust in the Lord with all thine heart; and lean not unto thine own understanding. In all thy ways acknowledge him and he shall direct thy paths. Be not wise in thine own eyes: fear the Lord, and depart from evil (Proverbs 3:5-7).

For He shall give His angels charge over thee, to keep thee in all thy ways (Psalms 91:11).

Chapter 1
Trust

September 11, 2001

The sun rose and the sky cleared.
Then we heard the devastating news.
We will never forget that beautiful blue-cloudless day.

Later, wearing work clothes and nasty shoes,
I ducked into Anderston Mill Road Baptist Church.
I took off my shoes upon arrival,
Walked down the aisle in stocking feet, sat down, and
Prayed with a church brimming with strangers.

I prayed for our country and
For what was to become of our family.

Fear drove me inside and
Comfort walked me out,
For I was reassured and confident Who was in charge.
It was indeed good to have been in the house of the Lord.

The Fourth of July Saga Continues

We usually are not a dramatic household; however, most years something extra out of the ordinary and large happens around the week of the fourth. The Thursday before the fourth this year, I had fed the orchids and was alone in the house with the pets. Just before dark, I grabbed Bella's red leash and she flipped into puppy mode. She took off running to play hide and seek. I walked upstairs and clipped the lead onto her collar and she was ready to go on the walkabout. Somehow, as we were going down the four hardwood steps to the foyer, I stepped on the leash and fell backwards. Seeing stars, I hurt my back, right hip, right ribs and right palm. Over the weekend I thought surely this would get better, but no. Terrified of falling again and not being able to get up and having to go straight from the hospital to assisted living, I feared I had cracked something important that would not grow back.

Jim was off work and we went to the doctor on Monday for an exam and x-rays. The nurse asked if I was allergic to anything other than shellfish and codeine and I said, "Yes, carbs - I break out in fat." As the x-ray tech was working, she sympathized and said it is hard to get over a fall and before she could comment on me being a "woman of a certain age", I interjected, "Yes, because I am no longer a spring chicken." Thank the good Lord nothing was broken. My trust in guardian angels paid off! I could have easily broken my neck or the good hip.

As I write this today, July 16, our grandson Wade turns twenty-two years old. The Monday after the Fourth, he was scammed and hacked - initially losing the money he earned so far this summer. We are positive the credit union's fraud department and the city police are doing their best. Recovery chances are slim; however, because he acted immediately and it is evident the bad actors kept trying multiple times to access his account after he froze it, there is a little hope. Hard life-lessons are emotionally and financially expensive.

Lay not up for yourselves treasures upon earth, where moth and rust doth corrupt, and where thieves break through and steal: But lay up for yourselves treasures in heaven, where neither moth nor rust doth corrupt, and where thieves do not break through nor steal: For where your treasure is, there will your heart be also (Matthew 6:19-21).

What is in store for us next Fourth of July? Only the Lord knows and nothing surprises Him.

Empty Nest
Tuesday, August 8, 2023

I did not cry because Wade was leaving. I cried because Jim took the time from his busy day to get up with us at 3 a.m. and help Wade into the airport at 4:06 a.m.. I could not bear the thought of letting Wade out onto the sidewalk and driving away alone. I was comforted to know he checked in and his big heavy bags were paid for, all was well, in order, and underway. This was the best sendoff we could give him.

Making it to his gates on time, and to be confident of his connections, would be next. The flight to Charlotte landed at 6:35 a.m. and his connecting flight departed at 7:00 a.m. leaving him and other passengers in Charlotte. They were finally able to leave at 11:24 a.m. and arrived in Phoenix at 4:21 p.m. our time.

His new life has begun. He will have to get organized because orientation starts this Friday and acclimate himself to the weather. It is currently 106 degrees in Tempe, Arizona. He ran 26.2 miles by himself this past Sunday and we were exceedingly concerned. Running that far with others, and with EMS along the way, is totally different. I do not even want to know it when he runs 26.2 miles again. Now will be the time to man-up and parent himself – still covered in prayer with occasional care packages.

What will I do with extra time on my hands? Stick to the routine, pray, volunteer more, and hopefully keep a cleaner house. And to rest assured Wade is protected by the good Lord sending His guardian angels to take charge over him.

Heart's Desire

I had an unrealistic expectation.

Totally out of my

Control and

Beyond all my power to reason.

Totally a monumental colossal mistake.

I learned the hard way through

Disappointment to

Rest content and trust.

1. Hope deferred maketh the heart sick: but when the desire cometh, it is a tree of life (Proverbs 13:12).

2. …ye have not, because ye ask not (James 4:2).

3. …for your Father knoweth what things ye have need of, before ye ask Him (Matthew 6:8).

4. Every good gift and every perfect gift is from above… (James 1:17).

5. Delight thyself also in the Lord: and He shall give thee the desires of thine heart (Psalms 37:4).

6. But seek ye first the kingdom of God and His righteousness; and all these things shall be added unto you (Matthew 6:33).

The Mask

People put on their masks

Go out to face the world, run their jobs and manage their homes.

Is the real self when you are naked or asleep?

Do you feel all alone in the world with a broken heart?

Heart sick then physically sick?

Drop the mask.

Pray and unburden yourself. Have a good cry. Get it all off your chest.

Trust that Jesus is listening and that he cares for you more than he cares for the sparrows he feeds every day.

Trust Him to help you.

He will never let you down.

Therefore if any man be in Christ, he is a new creature: old things are passed away; behold; all things are become new (2 Cor. 5:17).

...for the Lord thy God...go with thee; he will not fail thee, nor forsake thee (Deut. 31:6c).

I will not leave you comfortless: I will come to you (John 14:18).

...I will pour out my spirit unto you, I will make known my words unto you (Prov.1:23 b).

...Let not your heart be troubled, neither let it be afraid (John 14:27b).

Remain Calm

Ask yourself if this situation is worth having a heart attack over?

Are you willing to die on this hill?

Never underestimate your intelligence or overestimate other's intelligence.

Extend loving kindness to yourself.

Extreme and intense trust leads to confidence.

Stop trying and start trusting.

"Remember to let nothing disturb the calm peace of your soul."

St. Teresa of Avila

For He hath delivered me out of all trouble (Psalms 54:7a).

Dearly beloved, avenge not yourselves, but rather give peace unto wrath: for it is written, "Vengeance is mine: I will repay," saith the Lord (Romans 12:19).

The Beauty of Letting Go – Not Giving Up

Joan was a friend of mine in Lexington, South Carolina. She and her husband had six grown children and only one teenage daughter still lived at home. He had a powerful job in Columbia and left Joan for a pretty younger woman. Joan was devastated. They had a large beautiful home, country club membership, and status. She had not worked outside of the home since they married forty-years earlier. In the divorce, she lost her heavily mortgaged home, new vehicle, and perceived status. She moved into a two-bedroom apartment with the youngest daughter and bought a small used car. Humiliation and despair had overtaken her life and her countenance had soured.

She related the following story. Joan was an Episcopalian and went to her minister for counseling and poured out her broken heart. This was his advice: "Joan, do you see the massive beams overhead in our sanctuary? Let's pretend there is a large basket on the floor. Your ex-husband steps inside and sits down in the basket. You tie a rope securely to the handles and throw the rope up and over one of the sturdy beams in the ceiling. Now, with all your strength and with God's help, pull, pull, and pull him up to the ceiling and tie off the rope. Lift him up to the Lord. Let go and let God deal with him. You have your self-respect and the love of your children. Give up your bitterness. This is only hurting you." She asked what to do if these feelings resurfaced to engulf her. Her minister advised to put him back in the basket and hoist him up again.

Joan found peace and changed her mind-set to cope with her new life because she traded in her weakness for God's strength. Don't give up and remain stuck in negative emotions. Let go and live.

A merry heart doeth good like medicine: But a broken spirit drieth the bones (Proverbs 17:22).

...But a wounded spirit, who can bear? (Prov. 18:14b).

I (Jesus) am come that they might have life, and that they might have it more abundantly (John 10:10b).

New Creatures

Our home is situated on a wooded lot in the city. We have the convenience of everything being no more that twelve-minutes away. On the katio out back, trains are heard rumbling through town, and it is amazing to hear the cicadas calling and answering one another. The tree frogs and crickets chirp louder as night deepens. All are very loud to be so small.

The municipal airport is nearby and planes can be spotted and heard. The whirling helicopter blades remind me of the nightly news, during the War in Vietnam, showing the numbers killed in the jungles.

As a child, Daddy took us fishing. I was charmed with the dragonflies – which are neither dragons nor flies. I studied them in flight and was enchanted. Occasionally in our yard now, I am fortunate enough to see one working at the raised vegetable garden beds to feast upon smaller insects. Surprisingly, helicopters were designed by studying the dragonflies hovering, flying forward, backward, up, and down. They are the fastest flying insect; able to dash about at thirty-five miles per hour. They spend years in the larvae stage, but only a few months as an adult. It takes twelve hours for their veined wings to unfold, elongate, and fully extend to harden once they have emerged.

I have always admired them and was delighted to win the bid on a beautiful reproduction lamp with dragonflies at an auction. Clara Driscoll started at Tiffany's in 1888 and became the Department Head of the Women's Glass Cutting division in 1892. She designed the majority of Tiffany's most popular lamps and is credited with inventing the dragonfly-lamp design with its intricate-organic patterns, harmonious-color palettes, and jewel-like stained glass. To the Japanese, the dragonfly symbolizes agility and power. The Chinese recognize them as symbols of prosperity, harmony, and good fortune.

The dragonfly molts seventeen times, shedding off its old self and becoming new. They are programmed to leave the darkness of the water and fly toward the light. Christians trust, grow, and leave their dark pasts behind. They face the light to accept, embrace, and celebrate their change into new creatures through Christ.

Others' Words of Wisdom On Trust
with
Earnest Expectation and Peace

...forgetting those things which are behind, and reaching forth unto those things which are before. I press toward the mark for the prize of the high calling of God in Christ Jesus (Philippians 3:13c, 14).

And be not conformed to this world: but be ye transformed by the renewing of your mind, that ye may prove what is that good, and acceptable, and perfect, will of God (Romans 12:2).

...for I have learned, in whatsoever state I am, therewith to be content (Phil. 4:11b).

But whoso harkeneth unto me shall dwell safely, And shall be quiet from fear of evil (Prov. 1:33).

"Let there be peace on earth and let it begin with me."

Jill Jackson-Miller

Chapter 2
Having Children and Adoption

Mother discovered the identity of her biological father during her teenage years. She told us she sought him out, but did not speak or reveal in any manner that she was his daughter. Mother observed and left. I wonder how she felt about this and how long she watched him. Was he at work or elsewhere? Did Mother feel like she favored him physically in any way? Was she proud of him or disgusted? Was it better that he never knew Mother existed?

Once, Mother said she wished, as a baby, she had been put up for adoption, to have a real family with a mother, father, and perhaps siblings.

Once Mother and Daddy married, she transferred the *family* desire to her household and attempted to make me perfect.

Once Mother realized trying to make me perfect was a total futile waste of her time, and not wanting to expend this effort and energy on my younger brother, Doug, Mother relaxed – somewhat.

Moses was adopted by Pharaoh's daughter. Jesus was adopted by his earthly father, Joseph. We are adopted into the family of God. Our Heavenly Father loves us. We are never alone. Even if we do not have an earthly father, God cherishes and values us through adoption. He provides strength, protection and is the perfect father and we are his precious children.

The Lord hath made all things for himself (Prov. 16:4a).

And will be a Father unto you, and ye shall be my sons and daughters, saith the Lord Almighty (2 Corinthians 6:18).

For in Him we live, and move, and have our being... For we are also his offspring (Acts 17:28).

...ye have received the Spirit of adoption whereby we cry, Abba, Father (Romans 8:15).

Do not be afraid to have children and /or adopt. The good Lord has taken care of us thus far. What would lead you to believe He would not continue his mercy and provisions to us as parents and to the generations to come? Lift your future children up in prayer and rest assured the Lord will protect them for you.

Children are the future of our country. Do not fear the government, feel defeated and be intimidated. Trust God. Believe in His promises. Be bold, brave and have courage. Know we are on the winning side. The victory is won through the precious shed blood of Jesus.

Encouragement

Encourage one another and build each other up
(1 Thessalonians 5:11).

You have a set of skills, talents, and abilities

That only you can bring to the

World.

Your most valuable assets are your time, your attention, and your attitude.

Cultivate gratitude, seek beauty everywhere,

Find joy, laugh, hug every day,

Perform random acts of kindness, and

Be prepared to be surprised.

You never know what good is working for you.

"Rome wasn't built in a day, but they were laying bricks every hour."

English playwright, John Heywood

"The system is greater than the goal. Focusing on your habits is more important than worrying about your outcomes."

James Clear, author of *Atomic Habits*

"Yesterday is history.

Tomorrow is a mystery.

Today is a gift.

That's why we call it 'the present.'"

Eleanor Roosevelt

Mother and Daddy were not very healthy or wealthy; however, they were absolutely the wisest people we ever knew. We were tremendously blessed to have this wonderful couple as our parents. We have modeled the success of their kind, long-suffering, encouraging natures.

This is the last photo Doug took of them on Mother's Day in 1995, before Daddy passed away. Daddy and Mother went to North Charleston before Doug and Laury built their home, and Daddy helped Doug pick out the lot they built on. In this photograph, Mother is sitting in the swing Doug made and hung in their oak tree in the backyard. This tree survived Hurricane Hugo, remains strong and stands near the marsh area on the Ashley River.  The Cooper River and Ashely River flow together into the Charleston Harbor and form the Atlantic Ocean.

So Teach Us to Number Our Days (Psalms 90:12a).

In the blink of an eye you are conceived.

In the blink of an eye the kitchen catches fire… again.

In the blink of an eye the load shifts on the dock and

You are covered with falling freight.

In the blink of an eye your child is grown, finishing university,

And off to graduate school… far out of state.

In the blink of an eye one wrong decision destroys

That which has taken a lifetime to build.

In the blink of an eye you pass from here into eternity.

Chapter 3

"Survival of the Fittest"

Herbert Spencer, 1864

Lonesome Dove

Our red-tailed hawk casts a large shadow over the yard as he cruises overhead. If you believe in good luck, and one crosses your path, you will have peace and harmony. To the Native Americans, the hawk is a symbol of power, courage and strength.

Mr. Hawk is surveying his territory looking for prey of hopefully the nuisance variety. Meals of rabbit, bird, mouse, woodchuck, snake, and fish or lizard from the creek below the tree line are always on the menu. They are able to see prey from 100 feet in the air (ten stories high) and dive at up to 120 mph to catch it. They rest at night with their heads tucked into their fluffed-up feathers. We have found them resting atop our utility poles. They mate for life and hunt once in the morning and once in the afternoon. Eggs, nestlings, and young hawks are prey for the larger hawks, eagles, great horned owls, raccoons, fox and snakes. Daily, we hope no kitten or puppy is included for their snack.

Our next-door neighbor, Nora, told us a story of comforting a lonesome dove on her patio. All of a sudden, out of nowhere, our hawk swooped down making a meal of her new little friend. With feathers flying, all she could do was cry.

We are part of nature just like the plants and animals. The plants are pre-programmed, and the animals have instinct. We are given intuition, conscience, and the power of choice.

Luci Lu

Jim was working in Lexington, South Carolina, and stayed overnight at the Holiday Inn Express on Highway 378. He spotted this little female "tuxedo" feline with a tipped left ear. He fed her a chicken tender and she stole his heart.

On his next trip to Lexington, he saw her again and sent me the photo below. We decided, if he could catch her, he would bring her home to meet Oscar. He purchased a cardboard pet carrier and easily put her inside. She cried and he reassured her that she was alright all ninety miles home. Next day, I took her to the vet and she had a microchip. We contacted the microchip company and informed them she had been found. They let us know the person that trapped and chipped her had been notified and we would hear in a few weeks if she needed to be returned or if she was free to be adopted. They never responded, the time limit expired and we officially adopted another *tuxedo*.

'Lil Babe

Last summer, at the end of our street, our neighbor, Jane was caring for four indoor cats ranging from one to sixteen years of age. Early one morning, Pat, another neighbor, was helping Jane feed approximately eight kitties outside, when Jane's front door opened, in ran a tiny gray male tabby kitten with white mittens and white-sock hind feet. Pat finally found him in Jane's back bedroom and managed to catch him. She sat and held him for a long time. Jane did not think Pat would be able to give him up, but there is a no cat policy at MaMarie's house.

Pat put him in a crate for Jane and called me to see if we would foster him until Jane could find him a home. Of course, we said yes, and Wade and I went straight to Jane's to pick him up. Instead of fostering him, we decided to keep him.

I changed 'Lil Babe to Baby (pronounced Bay Bee) and Jim and Wade call him BC for Baby Cat. Since then, two of his siblings have also grown up and his twin had kittens of her own this year.

We have had him for a year now and he weighs almost twelve pounds. He is big, strong and exceedingly brave.

Our Foster Kittens

Nora and I took a litter of kittens from Bunny Bishop, our neighbor who rescues and feeds cat colonies for SFA (Speak for Animals). Their mother and one sibling had met an untimely demise. We adopted out Angel the grey one to an elderly couple in Huntersville, North Carolina. The wife suffers with COPD and the husband cares of her. Angel scratched the lady and having thin skin, Angel was tearfully returned because we have a 100% Satisfaction Guarantee Return Policy. Tommie, the black and white tuxedo had a twin, Timmie, and he went to live with Nora's sister and her husband early on in Huntersville too. The two black kittens, Suzette and Sammie, are together and happy with a local family.

We support Bunny in her efforts and agree with SFA's philosophy: "…enhancing the lives by providing access to free and low cost spray and neuter programs. Spraying and

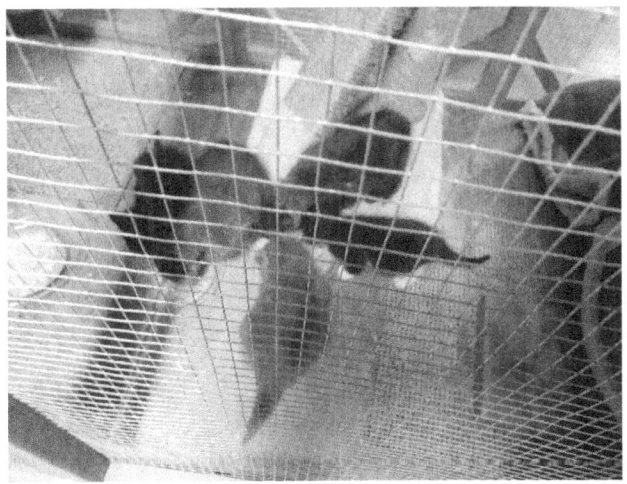 neutering reduces pet overpopulation, keeps unwanted animals out of shelters, limits the risk of certain health problems, and prevents euthanasia."

Our Furry Friends

The Felines

Our cats chatter intently watching the birds on the utility wires.

Well-fed and cared for, they still prowl for prey.

Graceful in their movements and

Usually calm and relaxed,

They stretch and play between naps, dining and grooming.

It is a joy to share our life with them and we are thankful

For their good health, company and sweet affection.

Angel and Tommie at 7-months old

The Canine

Bella, our Golden Retriever, will be nine-years old in October.

Becoming white in her muzzle and slower on walks,

She occasionally leaps into puppy mode.

Off we go around the circular driveway or

Around the block with our neighbor friends.

Our Bella is a quiet, warm, soft companion.

Fire Ants are Aptly Named

The weather was most pleasant as Bella and I walked up to Nora's next door neighbors' house. Marie, Pat and Isaiah were to join us for the morning walkabout around the block.

There is a massive magnolia tree on their property line and it has never bloomed on Nora's side. Once in their driveway, among the lower branches I spied a single huge blossom. In awe, I came closer to inspect the inner flower and to hopefully catch a whiff of its intoxicating fragrance. About 2 seconds later, pain engulfed both feet and lower legs. Instead of paying attention, I was distracted to admire the bloom and found myself on top of a fire ant hill.

Screaming, "Help, Help, Help," Marie, Pat, and Isaiah rushed out thinking I had fallen (again). To their surprise the fire ants were stinging and clinging on for dear life. I became more unbalanced bending over attempting to take off my shoes while swatting the ants away.

This girl was on fire!

Isaiah dashed to get a chair, Marie ran to get the agave nectar, and Pat rushed out with Benadryl tablets. In less than five minutes, now shoeless, I was a fully medicated sticky mess. Pat brought wet bath cloths and Marie grabbed some sandals. They sent me home with my shoes in a to-go bag along with more Benadryl, Neosporin, and homeopathic calendula cream.

Their first aid worked. I nursed my feet and legs during the day and was able to go on the evening walkabout pain free.

One cannot put a price on friendship and good neighbors. Treasure them.

"No one has ever become poor by giving."

Anne Frank

Just Passing Through
Monday 7/24/2023, 6:58 a.m.

Surrounded by the misty morn,

Heard the Canadian geese honking

Before seeing five in flight formation.

Are they headed home further south,

Looking for water in the numerous lakes and ponds nearby,

Or are they part of the new resident population?

Worm Bed or Compost Pile

As Daddy cleared out the back of our double lot at our home on Robin Hood Drive in the 1950's, he created a worm bed on the sunny right side before the tree line. He frequently layered newspapers, kitchen scraps, and leaves. He fed and watered it; therefore, the soil was alive with microorganisms. He gave and received.

Whenever Daddy and my brother, Doug, went crappie fishing, all they had to do was peel back the top layer of the bed and voila free red wigglers for the trip. Some years, we were excited to see volunteer tomato plants producing free heirloom home grown tomatoes. Small spaces can produce much to appreciate.

So neither he who plants nor he who waters is anything, but only God who gives the growth (1 Corinthians 3:7).

The Oncidium

Our Phalaenopsis orchid collection is thoroughly enjoyed for its stamina and beauty. Nora brought me the first one while in knee rehab and the second one was rescued off her back porch.

Eyeing an oncidium in a florist shop, I was enchanted with its exquisite feathery blossoms. After sleeping on it, next day, I made it mine. Our cats were enchanted also and virtually destroyed its foliage immediately before the oncidium could be rescued and isolated. It has been repotted, fed weakly weekly and now sits in a sturdy thrifted basket from Wellspring Treasures. It grew new pseudo bulbs and leaves; however, failed to bloom for three years, probably due to the shocks and stresses.

This June, surprisingly, up popped a single flower spike and buds. Last week it started blooming, and today I brought it to Wellspring. On the sales tag, it is noted: "Oncidium - Upcycled4Charity" - No Cats. Our plants sell quickly there and hopefully, the oncidium will soon find a new home with someone who will cherish it and have more success in getting it to bloom again next year.

The flowers appear on the earth; the time of the singing of birds is come, and the voice of the turtle is heard in our land (Song of Solomon 2:12).

"Bloom where you are planted."
Bishop of Geneva, Saint Francis de Sales (1567-1622).

All Things Great and Small

Two weeks ago, erratically crossing our back yard, heading west was what I thought to be a rabid coyote. It was pitiful – so scrawny, stumbling and confused. I called the non-emergency 911 number and they said they would contact the Wildlife Department.

Nora's next-door neighbor, Pat had seen her soon thereafter and thought it was a female red fox with mange. She called Wildlife and they were to send Pat some medicine. One dose would help 60% and two doses would help 90%. Pat's son Isaiah took it upon himself to name her Jellybean and they have fed and watered her every day.

Yesterday, as Bella and I stepped out for the first stroll, she was startled and perked up her ears before I saw Jellybean walking out from beside our house. Jellybean meandered through the front yard, crossed the street and on to the left side of the cottage across the way. She headed on towards a home beyond that is known for helping feed the neighborhood cats. Jellybean was walking confidently, seemed less under-nourished and the coat looked a little bit thicker. The neighbors stay on the lookout for her, reporting to Pat for the Wildlife Department. The City Police told us there was nothing they could do about Jellybean unless she was being destructive or aggressive.

With all the new construction nearby, the wild animal's habitats are being destroyed and they have nowhere to go except into the old neighborhoods with woods and creeks. This year, we have seen many more raccoons than usual and for the first time, observed several woodchucks grazing on lawns and ducking into rain drains as vehicles pass by.

Remember the baby turtles that hatch and make their way to the sea and the ant that can carry twenty times their body's weight? All creatures have value and a purpose. They help maintain our environment by pollinating, eating pests and scavenging among other talents. The insects and undomesticated animals wake up and eat that which the Lord has provided. Humans are born, learn to crawl, walk, and speak. They grow and go to school, get an education and train to be able to get a job. Then they earn money so they can sit down and eat.

Miss Cecil Frances Humphries was born in April, 1818 in Dublin Ireland. She based her beautiful and famous poem All *Things Bright and Beautiful* which was first published in 1848 on Psalms 104:24. She married Mr. William Alexander in October of 1850 and died In October 1895. The lyrics to her first verse are:

"All things bright and beautiful, all things great and small. All things wise and wonderful, 'twas God that made them all."

For every beast of the forest is Mine, And the cattle upon a thousand hills. I know all the fowls of the mountains and the wild beasts of the fields are Mine (Psalms 50:10-11).

Awareness

Walking the dogs with our neighbors at least twice a day is an anticipated pleasure. We enjoy adult chit chat, the company of our pups, and the weather, except during thunder or extremes. Most outings, the stroll is over too quickly; we part and look forward to meeting again soon. During longer walkabouts with Bella, I notice the sky, lovely flowers, and lush green lawns with active animals chattering. In the evening during the last walk of the day, hopefully, the moon and stars will be on full display. Studying the moon, it skips around the night sky and I never know where to find it next.

One evening, this past winter, as we were arriving back at the front door, I peered up through a leafless oak tree to see a brilliant crescent moon high in the west glowing through the branches. This quiet peaceful scene reminded me to be in awe of the Maker of the ever-changing seasons.

Chapter 4
Seasons

Senses

As you allow yourself to be immersed in nature,

Be calm as the gentle dew upon the grass.

Pay close attention your senses.

See the vibrant colors,

Hear the sounds of the birds and squirrels by day,

The crickets, owls, and foxes by night.

Smell the honeysuckle, fresh cut grass or new-mown hay.

Avoid the rose's thorn and pet your animal's soft fur.

Taste the freshly picked ripe fruit of your labor.

You Do Not Have to Shovel Sunshine

Living in the piedmont of South Carolina, we are fortunate to have pleasant weather most of the year. We have experienced the effects of only two tornados. Hurricanes off the coast bring us extra rain and wind. The dog days of summer are humid and hot; however, not unbearable. The atmosphere feels invigorating when walking out onto the porch during or after a rain storm to breathe in the negative ions. This crisp cool comforting gift is from God. The spring and autumn are exceedingly beautiful and at the first glimpse of a snowflake in winter, most are delighted. Usually, when snow falls it melts shortly thereafter and when the temperature stays low enough, the children revel in their snow days. Of all the weather that comes our way, being able to stare up into the gently falling snow is magical and my favorite.

The weather affects some people negatively. A cloudy sky or a foggy day dampens their spirits. Never able to justify weather as an excuse, I counter the moaning and groaning with giving thanks for the rain and the fact that it helps keep down fires when people insist on burning leaves and/or brush.

We pray for those in the path of the storm and remember – it always stops.

Spring

As the cheerful pansies and vintage camellia blossoms remain,

The purple crocus and first daffodils appear.

Then the tulips and Carolina Yellow Jessamine burst forth in February.

Mid-spring we can smell the honeysuckle,

Then the cherry trees try to outdo one another.

The azaleas and dogwoods always bloom for Easter, and

The fragrant wisteria drapes across the trees and utility lines

in May.

My favorite is the thrift Jim planted for me

In shades of pink, blue, and lavender that cascade over our rock wall.

Morning

Breathe in the fresh air and appreciate an azure sky.

Be restored, strengthened, and soothed.

Feel grounded, clear minded, and relaxed.

Sufficiently refreshed; go master your day!

"Nature itself is the best medicine."

Hippocrates

"Look deep into nature, and then you will understand everything better."

Albert Einstein

Be still, and know that I am God (Psalms 46:10a).

Summer
Morning 4 a.m.

The moon is setting covered with hazy clouds.

You finished sinking into the horizon on the way into

Our manicured Greenville/ Spartanburg Airport.

I have never seen more impressive grounds.

Bless you, talented landscape architects and Roger Milliken,

for your environmental passion and love of the "Noble Trees."

Later on, I saw the breeze affect the tops of our trees, on
flowers and blades of grass and felt its kiss on my skin.
Hummingbirds come to the hostas, as butterflies and bees feast
on nectar inside the blossoms on the tomato and pepper plants
in the raised garden beds. Happy early birds sang, the
neighbor's roses were in full bloom and the blue hydrangeas
were heavy with their heads drooping down from last night's
rain.

The back yard has a gentle slope down to the creek. The
trees have never been cut and the wild weeping cherry,
magnolia and dogwoods thrive with the mature hardwoods and
pines. I have wondered many times what could be seen and
heard if monkeys were playing and swinging to-and-fro in the

trees beyond the safety of our long narrow broken tiled screened in katio.

We do not know where the wind comes from or where it goes - even so, we are grateful for the momentary coolness. July and August are hot and steamy months. As a few yellow leaves flutter to the ground, I am thankful and encouraged. Just as our Heavenly Father provided a rainbow promise, so the falling of a few more yellow leaves holds His promise of cool crispy days ahead.

Sunset

Tuesday, June 27, 2023, 6:40 p. m.

The sun swirled white within yellow as it slowly sank

And

Was momentarily surprisingly red as it dipped out of view.

The stately green trees and alabaster sky calmly remained still,

As last ray of sunset whispered,

"Goodnight, hope to see you in the morning!"

Southern Summers

Thursday, July 6, 2023, 7:17 a. m.

As the blinding blazing white hot sun rises the east,

Sending forth angular rays toward the west,

The remaining misty fog in the valley is slowly burning off.

Welcome to summer in the south!

Asiatic Lily bulbs are over 25-years old.

Isaiah Luker's arm is 13-years old

The Face of Morning

Monday, July 17, 2023, 6:54 am

The sun rose huge and neon orange.

The eerie solid light dolphin gray sky caused by the wildfires was ominous.

Within minutes, the sun was higher and the orange had lost its sharpness and

Dark-slate gray cirrus clouds skirted across

The face of the morning.

Autumn

Sunday, November 20, 2022, 5:20 pm

The sunset is glorious!

Giant blue-cotton-candy swaths shine through the peach-sherbet backdrop

To overtake the western sky.

Toward the north, the colors mute and

In the east, night is falling.

Dogwood Trees are Multi-Talented

Their white flowers from spring loosen in the breeze,

And green leaves appear for summer.

Finally relieved of the sweltering-humid heat,

They show off brilliantly for fall.

Their glossy-red berries attract the winter songbirds

And later the moon is able to shine through the barren branches.

Winter

Standing under billions of stars overhead.

And billions of snowflakes underfoot;

I see the snow gingerly clinging to our holly bushes and evergreen trees.

Knowing all are made by the same hand of our Father in heaven,

I breathe in the fresh frigid air and exhale to see my breath and remember life is like a vapor.

While the earth is sleeping, readying itself for rebirth,

I quietly step out onto the new fallen snow.

Looking up into the cloudless ebony sky, and

Seeing the distant moon and luminous stars,

In the hushed calm silence, I am one with nature.

Chapter 5

Therapy

Water Therapy

When our grandson, Wade, was a very little boy, and after a big and tiring day at school, he was sometimes cranky. I would *throw* him into his bath tub filled with bubbles and plastic toys. Often we would go over Bible memory verses or a spelling list for a while as he would play, splash, and enjoy the warm comfort.

During the spring break of Wade's junior year in high school, I took him and his friend Theo on a short cruise. One day while they were playing basketball on the deck, I was in the spa area basking in the sun. It seemed we were on top of the world with water 360 degrees around us. The Caribbean Sea was peaceful and I felt protected by our loving Creator. We were together, alone, with water below and heaven above - suspended in space and time.

Music Therapy

Wade often played the piano for our friends and relatives in assisted living.

We witnessed:

Tapping toes

Clapping hands

Singing along

Smiles and

Joy.

Cost: Personal Time and Energy

Value: Priceless

"When words fail, music speaks."
Hans Christian Anderson

The Lord thy God in the midst of thee is mighty; he will save, he will rejoice over thee with joy; he will rest in his love, he will joy over thee with singing (Zephaniah 3:17).

Retail Therapy

Charity shops win hands down. My weekly thrifting budget maxes out at $20.00. While volunteering at Wellspring Treasures, and Habitat for Humanity, I pop into their showrooms seeking a few amazing surprises and usually buy candles for the katio - we burn at least twenty most nights. We furnished the entire katio last year for a total of $160.00 from charity shops, and only need a few candles every week or so to keep it glowing. Occasionally a bargain can be found for "Upcycle4Charity". It is fun to turn someone's donation into someone else's treasure to resell or to donate the finer pieces to Habitat or Hatcher Gardens for their auctions.

We are thankful for our katio which is a small beautiful peaceful space. In the mornings, I read the Bible my parents gave me when I was eight years old. It was falling apart and Jim had it rebound twenty years ago. Always including at least one Proverb for wisdom (there are 31), I study, write, and pray that I would understand what He meant by what He said. Out there every evening, I access how the day unfolded and answer these questions in my journal:

1. What was the coup du jour - the surprise?
2. Find anything exciting to up cycle?
3. Three good things that happened today.
4. Three things for which to be grateful.
5. Mistakes?

6. Improvements?
7. Lessons learned?

Pet Therapy

Experiencing affection, comfort, and unconditional love wrapped in warm soft fur promotes calmness and is reported to reduce blood pressure.

"When I needed a hand I found your paw."
                                                        Author unknown

"No one appreciates the very special genius of your conversation as the dog (or cat) does."
                                                        Christopher Morley

"I have found that when you are deeply troubled, there are things you get from the silent devoted companionship of a dog that you can get from no other source."
                                                        Doris Day

Couples Therapy

Spouse to counselor: "What if he/ she does that again?"

Counselor to couple: "You will not die."

Chapter 6

How I Lost 55 Pounds in 10 Months
on Keto with Intermittent Fasting

The right knee was replaced in May, I had major melanoma surgery near the left ankle in November and the left knee was replaced the following May. Recovery was a nightmare. I took so many Aleve my family doctor said I had kidney damage. Rehabilitation was awful and severely depressing. It is not that I regret getting the new knees, quite the contrary; otherwise, I would have been in a wheelchair on heavy pain meds if I had not lost my mind. I had gained up to weigh over two hundred pounds and my orthopedic doctor said I now needed a new left hip. All this pain, no energy, no enthusiasm… was I dying? There was no way to face a new hip at this weight and with this attitude.

9/12/2022 at 205 lbs.

Monday, October 24, 2022, was the day of reckoning - the date of the breaking point. I baked my second cake in one week and realized I was digging my own grave with a sugar spoon. I had had it! I was disgusted with weighing the most in my life. Enough was enough. I gave up sugar, which meant sweet tea, and Pepsi, too, and went back on the Atkins Diet (again). My Gaffney friend, Nancy Krugle, introduced me to Dr. Eric Berg on YouTube where I learned more about Keto, and something new to me - Intermittent Fasting. I stopped snacking and had three meals a day. After a few weeks I dropped back to two meals a day and after a few more weeks, I cut back to one meal a day (OMAD). Usually, I have strawberries with cream cheese, two eggs and sausage or bacon, or vegetable soup with chicken or ham, or a chef salad. I especially enjoy a grilled rib-eye steak, or grilled skirt steak and onions at Mexican restaurants. My favorite meal is homemade French onion soup with no crouton and left over steak in the bottom of the bowl plus extra mozzarella or provolone cheese melted on top. You will save money by eating less and cooking more at home.

Supper is at six p.m.; however, my eating window is from 2 p.m. until 6:30 p.m. It is best to eat at least three hours before bedtime and I try not to drink much late in the day to reduce nighttime bathroom trips; therefore, lowering the risk of falling and breaking something important that will not grow back.

On Wednesday November 23, 2022 I baked the final cake for our next-door neighbor, Nora's 79th birthday. After turning out the cake to cool, I washed the Bundt pan, dried it, and put it in the donate box for Habitat.

I enjoy healthy oils, nature's carbs not manmade carbs, and try to avoid heavily processed chemically-laden foods. The exception is micro waved pepperoni with shredded whole milk mozzarella cheese for a rare 10 p.m. snack.

When tempted to take a bite of the forbidden fruit, remember Abraham Lincoln's sage advice:

"Discipline is choosing between what you want now and what you want most."

Keep track of your weekly progress. The scale is not your enemy; it is only a tool. Please do not weigh every day because you may get mad and eat things you shouldn't. Stay glad you are on the right track to become healthier. You can feel your clothes loosening and that is sufficient until the scale catches up. Weigh on the same day each week. If you are really unhappy about what you see, be extra good that day, weigh the next morning and if you are happier, post that number in your tracker.

From Jennifer L. Scott with *The Daily Connoisseur*, I learned more about Intermittent Fasting and saw her interview with Dr. Mindy Pelz. From Jennifer's podcasts and Dr. Pelz's book, *Fast Like a Girl*, I understand our hormones better in light of the benefits of fasting – especially on mental clarity.

Friday, May 2, 2023… Mother's Day weekend… last year this week I weighed 205 pounds and still stood five feet two inches tall. It took me two days, two four-hour naps, and a week of sore muscles to get over cleaning our broken tiled screened in katio. This day, in two hours and forty-two pounds lighter, I did the same work with no naps and no sweating. Hallelujah!

Through the grace of God and absorbing and applying the knowledge of others, I am grateful for the information, the power and the strength to take control of my food choices.

May 2, 2023 at 163 lbs.

"Let food be thy medicine and medicine be thy food."

Hippocrates

"Eat to live not live to eat."

Benjamin Franklin

He causeth the grass to grow for the cattle, And herb for the service of man: that he may bring forth food out of the earth… (Psalms 104:14 a, b).

"Starve your distractions and feed your focus."

Daniel Goleman

For no man ever yet hated his own flesh; but nourisheth and cherisheth it… (Ephesians 5:29).

8/17/2023 at 150 lbs. with my first book
A Five and Dime's Million-Dollar Baby

Chapter 7
Minimalism

"Don't let the perfect be the enemy of good."

Voltaire, 1770

"…progress and only progress."

Dana K. White, 2021

Overwhelming is not the word for it. We dealt with Mother's seventy-two years' worth of household items after she passed away. We had to face clearing out Jim's Aunt Biddies' home in Seneca before she went into assisted living and then again deal with her possessions after she died at Thanksgiving in 2020.

Raised during the depression, they had a scarcity mindset due to the state of the country and rationing. They never recovered from their fear of shortages. Daddy kept rubber bands, paper clips and a big ball of string. He could fix almost anything with those three simple supplies. Biddie never threw away a mayonnaise jar or any old medicine. Mother told us that during this time, her grandmother, Elzie cut cardboard to line her shoes.

It is amazing how little we actually need. When going on a trip, we take the essentials. How would it feel to have your home de-cluttered to the point that stepping through your front door would feel like returning to a tidy, inviting, cozy hotel room decorated with your personality.

It is possible and you can do it. *Better* is the goal.

1. Do not tackle the garage, attic or sentimental items first.

2. Have a large black trash bag, and donate boxes at the ready.

3. Start small. Clean out your vehicle. Clean out your wallet. Clean off your front porch and entryway.

4. Have a "No-Go Zone" such as the entry table because a flat surface tends to collect junk-visual noise. Keep it simple and reflect your style with a special lamp or a cherished piece of art. Commit to keeping one surface clutter free daily for a week and see how you feel.

5. Consider adopting the 20/20 rule for "just in case items". If you can replace an item for $20.00 in less than 20 minutes let it go.

We love antiques and especially tiger oak. I have a hall tree I purchased in West Columbia and had it delivered to Spartanburg in 1990. Later on Jim and I bought a tiger-oak chaise lounge with dreadful brown upholstery at an auction. Years later, Mr. Mims in Wellford recovered it magnificently in burgundy fabric with wandering golden African animals. These two items are my prized possessions. If we ever had to move, those would be the two *must haves* on the moving van.

The few oriental objects we enjoy evoke mystery and beauty through their delicate intricate designs. These thrifted objects of art include a lamp here, a vase there and planters utilized indoors and then outdoors on the katio during warmer weather. I have wondered about the artisans who created these pieces we treasure. Was nature the inspiration for their color and material choices? Will they ever know their efforts have been richly and fully appreciated?

My neighbors are generous, especially with ice, food, clothing, household items, and kittens. Items flow in and out, house to house. We donate, purchase, purge, cook, shop, share, and repeat. Nora has donated many plant cuttings for me to continue growing, potting, and donating to Wellspring. It is fun and adds to the store's décor before the plants are sold.

Choose one day a week to launder your personal clothes. The basic uniform of the day requires no thinking or stress in the morning. You love everything in your closet because it is interchangeable, comfortable, fits well, is presentable and in good repair. I usually wear black because it is easy. I have a black suede jacket that Jim brought me from Mexico at least thirty-five years ago. My red raincoat is still in great condition after twenty years. Daddy taught us to take care of our things and they would last.

I embrace the Scandinavian Concept of Hygge — to be cozy, comfy, and content. In the front room we have a cat tree at the window, plush blankets, pillows and multiple cat beds. On the katio we have soft chairs, cushions and tons of candles all curated from charity shops. I dare Southern Living, since they started publishing in 1966, to recall a photo of a cozier katio totally furnished for $160.00.

I read *The Gentle Art of Swedish Death Cleaning* written by Margareta_Magnusson, and learned "how to free yourself and your family from a lifetime of clutter". Do it yourself before others have to do it for you. "A loved one wishes to inherit nice things from you. Not all things from you."

After I discovered minimalism, I downsized everything that was mine. After my clothes, I cleaned out the hall closet. It felt so freeing. After de-cluttering and donating, I was mentally able and ready to start organizing.

Enough is a mindset. We are not going to make it out alive. The death rate is 100%. Appreciate what the Lord has provided while we are here. To be a good steward, it is easier with less.

For we brought nothing into the world, and it is certain we can carry nothing out (1Timothy 6:7).

Now… buy the orchids.

Light the candles.

Wear your best.

Use the cloth napkins,

And perhaps,

Adopt one more cat.

In a nutshell: Is the item beautiful and/or useful? If yes, keep it where you would look for it first; if not, donate it (Habitat will it pick-up). If broken, repair or discard it. Learn to say "No." Minimize your home and your calendar to keep from being overwhelmed. Devote yourself to what really matters – time to invest in people – not wasting time controlling vast possessions.

With references, I am able to coach you through this. Please contact me if you need a push in the downsizing direction. Until then, my best sources to recommend for information, inspiration and encouragement on Minimalism are: *The More of Less,* by Joshua Becker, and two podcasts by Dawn Madsen, *The Minimal Mom*, and Dana K. White, *A Slob Comes Clean*.

The charity shops are where your excess belongings go when you declutter, downsize and/or die. These charities know how to process your items for the greatest benefit for others.

Wellspring Treasures Staff and Volunteers

Volunteering with the staff of Habitat for Humanity

Other's Words of Wisdom on Minimalism

"The height of sophistication is simplicity."

Clare Booth Luce (1931)

"Less is more."

Architect, Ludwig Mies van der Rohe (1947)

"Our life is frittered away in detail…Simplify, simplify, simplify."

Henry David Thoreau

"Lead a simple life. First reduce your greed's. Then reduce your needs."

Rita Ghatourey

"In character, in manner, in style, in all things, the supreme excellence is simplicity."

Henry W. Longfellow

"The secret of happiness, you see, is not found in seeking more, but in developing the capacity to enjoy less."

Socrates
450 BC

Focus on what you can control.

Epictetus

Chapter 8
Breast Cancer

My grandmother, Molly WeHunt, Aunt Marie WeHunt and Mother-in-Law Mary Harden died of breast cancer.

In the 1980's I was in the bra business and fitted girls as young as eleven years old in DD bras. A friend in the bowling business at this same time said he had young ladies wearing 6-7-8 size bowling shoes and now they were wearing 8-9-10. What was going on? We deduced it must be the growth hormones and steroids in the foods these girls were ingesting. Since 1994 most tomato and other crops are GMO.

During my retail lingerie career, I spoke to civic clubs about Breast Cancer Awareness. I opened with these questions:

1. Who among you gentlemen ever had a mother? All hands would rise.

2. Who among you gentlemen ever had a grandmother, sister, wife, daughter, aunt or niece? All hands rose.

3. Who among you gentlemen have ever had a loved one die from breast cancer? Most hands rose.

4. Who among you gentlemen have ever encouraged your female loved ones to do monthly self-breast exams and

to get yearly checkups with mammograms? Very few hands were raised.

5. Who among you gentlemen can now promise to encourage your female loved ones to do so? All hands rose.

Mission accomplished. Those were amusing and surprising presentations for me and the club members. The Lord helped me remain calm and speak from the heart. Early detection saves lives.

Chapter 9
Blood

In 1978 I had a botched hysterectomy that required five units of blood. In recovery, high school friend Brenda Green was my RN and I remember her screaming, "Oh no! Her BP is falling." Next thing I knew, the oxygen mask was on and many hours later woke up in my hospital room. Thank the Good Lord and my guardian angel knew my son needed his mother.

Fortunately, my blood type is O Positive, and the critically needed blood was readily obtained. My husband, Jim, has type O Negative so he donates regularly. Quoting from The Red Cross: "Only 7% of the population is O Negative. However, the need for O negative blood is highest because it is used most often during emergencies." It is the safest blood for transfusions for immune deficient newborns and premature babies.

There is no substitute for human blood. Please give the gift of life.

Chapter 10
Questions Needing Answers

How to Adult?

1. Get a life. "To be interesting, be interested."

   Dale Carnegie

2. Do not be desperate for a mate.

3. "If you are walking on eggshells, you are walking with the wrong tribe."

   Pat Luker

4. If you need a best friend, adopt a dog. They see the truth and pain in you even when you are fooling everyone else and you will get plenty of exercise to boot.

Open Minded

Just because we disagree does not equal, I am stupid or evil. Are we not Americans? Are we not guaranteed the right to free speech? Is everyone not entitled to their opinion?

Are we self-righteous, arrogant and closed minded? Can we not be open to the possibility that we may be wrong? Is it possible to be persuaded with a new set of facts?

Be a lifelong learner. Search for truth. Do your homework, be informed. Be able to get off your high horse long enough to change your mind when convinced that is the right thing to do.

"The time is always right to do what is right."

Dr. Martin Luther King, Jr.

Instinctively, we naturally know the difference in right and wrong. Females have the advantage of women's intuition if/when they listen to it. Men use gut feelings to their advantage if/when they listen to it. The question is: are we listening?

"The more I learn, the more I realize how much I don't know."

Albert Einstein

More Bang for Your Buck

Orchids, especially, the phalaenopsis are the true bargain in fresh flowers. Bought in bloom; enjoy months of beauty. Repotting is easy to free their roots and feed them "weakly weekly". Near Thanksgiving a flower spike may start peeking through from under a second leaf and if you are exceedingly fortunate two flower spikes may appear. Expect your orchids to bud and bloom during the winter and spring. Some will remain beautiful beyond Labor Day. With a little care and medium sunlight, they will thrive and live for years and years and years.

You must put your affairs in order anyway, so go ahead and decide: Who will be written into your will to receive your orchid collection?

What Will You Leave Behind?

Money,

Material Possessions,

Debt or

Fond memories of you:

Sharing,

Helping, and

Making a difference?

What is Developing Your Child's Character?

Home training?

School environment?

Church teachings?

Friends' influence?

Heredity?

Nutrition?

Encouragement?

Prayer?

All the above?

"If all that I would want to do, would be to sit and talk to you…would you listen?"

Ann Ashford (and Matthew McConaughey, age twelve)

"Children learn by an adult's example, not by their words."

Carl Gustav Jung, Swiss psychiatrist and psychoanalyst (1875 – 1961)

What are your children's superpowers?

What are they good at and enjoy doing most often? These are gifts and talents from the Lord.

Even a child is known by his doings, whether his work be pure, and whether it be right (Proverbs 20:11).

Train up a child in the way he should go: and when he is old, he will not depart from it (Proverbs 22:6).

This last verse is a warning to us parents, not a promise. Our children are on loan to us for approximately 18 years. We are responsible to guide and direct them. Know when we stand at the judgment, we will be held to account.

Having Sex is Not for Sport

Normally, when male and female join, there is potential for new life to be formed in the image of God. That is heavy and seems serious enough to give people pause.

Once created, welcome the news as a blessing.

Will the baby become... a *decision*?

Life begins at conception, is a gift, and is God's plan.

"My Father Planned it All,"
Song written by Alfred B. Smith

I sing thro' the shade and sunshine,

And trust Him what'er befall;

His way is best – it leads to rest;

My Father planned it all.

...you knit me together in my mother's womb (Psalm 139:13 b).

Nothing Surprising, Anymore

1. When did it become socially acceptable to wear pajama bottoms and slippers anywhere except at home?

2. When did public displays of affection morph into more than holding hands and a quick kiss hello or goodbye?

3. Why do we have to make a five-minute appointment with a friend or family member to speak with them personally to garner their undivided attention?

Are You Ready?

Are you still chasing the big dream?

Is your heart fully prepared to lead your mind?

With your training and experience, are you now able to act?

For God hath not given us the spirit of fear; but of power and of love, and of a sound mind (2 Timothy 1:7).

"Live the life you've dreamed…None are so old as those who have outlived enthusiasm."

Henry David Thoreau

"The cave you fear to enter holds the treasure you seek."

Joseph Campbell

Fulfillment

Questions:

Dear Lord,

Why am I here?

What is my purpose?

What do you need me to do?

How can I fulfill my purpose for you letting me live during this particular time?

Answer:

Live your purpose in service to others.

Chapter 11
The Best Advice I Ever Received

1.   For whosoever shall call upon the name of the Lord shall be saved (Romans 10:13).

2.   ...Thou shalt love the Lord thy God with all thy heart, and with all thy soul, and with all thy mind....Thou shalt love thy neighbor as yourself (Matthew 22:37-39).

3.   Therefore all things whatsoever ye would that men should do to you, do ye even so to them... (Matthew 7:12a).

4.   "Apprentice yourself to a master for free. Save them time and learn their craft."

Robert Greene

5.   "Price is what you give. Value is what you get."

Warren Buffett

6.   Do the best you can with what you have to work with – seek additional training and mentors. "You are one decision away from heading in the right direction toward achieving your goal...Be grateful for those along the path that have loved and supported you."

Mel Robbins

7. "The best money advice ever given me was from my father. When I was a little girl, he told me, 'Don't spend anything unless you have to.' "

Dinah Shore

8. Give a portion to seven, yes also to eight (investments): for thou knowest not what evil shall be upon the earth (Ecclesiastes 11:2).

9. Model the Proverbs 31 woman who was diversified, hardworking, diligent, dignified, and helped those in need.

Grandmother's Advice on Worry

Worry is a total waste of time.

Worry is a total waste of your imagination.

Worry is a total lack of faith

In yourself,

In God, and

In His ability to help you.

Be careful (worry) for nothing; but in everything by prayer and supplication with thanksgiving let your requests be made known to God. And the peace of God, which surpasses all understanding, shall keep your hearts and minds through Christ Jesus (Philippians 4:6-7).

Grandmother's Advice on 1960's Sex Education

Do not do it for two reasons:

1. May get pregnant
2. May catch germs

The Truth:

What? Know ye not that your body is the temple of the Holy Ghost, which is in you, which ye have of God, and ye are not your own? For ye are bought with a price: therefore, glorify God in your body and in your spirit, which are God's. (I Cor. 6:19-20).

Grandmother's Advice to Young People

Sex is Safe in Marriage as Fire is Safe in the Fireplace

Remember mother is the coach and father is the judge, hopefully not a harsh judge. Pray with your parents for your future bride or groom that they would remain pure for you as you remain pure for them. It is intangible and the most beautiful wedding gift for one another. Marriage is special, private and holy. Choose wisely and plan to care, and be committed to each other.

Boys, maintain good friendships, be productive and helpful. Talk to your father about growing into manhood because your changing body is preparing you to become a father to bring new life into the world.

Girls, talk to your mothers about your cycle so it will not be a terrifying surprise. You are naturally transitioning from a child into a young lady. Hopefully you will remain at home under the protection of your parents until you have an education and career. Possibly marry and then have a family of your own.

Cast a wide net. Try different sports, musical instruments and have varied interests. One or two may develop into skills in which to excel and enjoy for a lifetime. Maintain worthy friendships, stay devoted to your family, and then one family at a time and one community at a time will lead to a healthier nation.

Children, obey your parents in the Lord: for this is right. Honor thy father and mother; which is the first commandment with promise. That it may be well with thee, and thou mayest live long on the earth. And, ye fathers provoke not your children to wrath: but bring them up in the nurture and admonition of the Lord (Ephesians 6:1-4).

Grandmother's Advice on Pre-Pre-Marital Counseling

If divorce is an option, stay single.

What kind of life do you want? Gentlemen, does she make you feel like a man or ladies, does he make you feel like a woman? Are you comfortable with yourself in their presence? Are they generous, kind and have good relationships with their parents? Most wives crave appreciation more than compliments. They want love, security, and a good father for their children. Husbands need to feel loved, appreciated and respected. Also to be intimate, enjoy great food and their wife be a good mother to their children – not necessarily in that order. Look for a mate that wants most of the same things you do. After deciding that Christ is your Savior, the second most important decision you will ever make is who you will marry.

Before you make an appointment with the clergy who will perform your ceremony, put the attraction and chemistry aside and discuss the following topics with your beloved to avoid pitfalls, mistakes, and serious unrealistic expectations. Also, iron out as much as possible in advance and prepare for detours around possible unnecessary chaos. It may be comforting to make your own list and hash those topics out before you meet with your counselor and take some of the questions with you to the appointment. Know being married will be a major adjustment for you both.

Faith: Do not be unequally yoked.

Prayer: Silently or aloud?

Money: No secrets.

              Same accounts or His, Hers, Ours?

              Get or stay debt free?

              Amount to save in the emergency fund?

              Budget or fly by the seat of your pants?

Children: How soon to start trying? How many? Open
              to adoption? Their education?

Family: Vacations alone together or with extended
              family?

              Holidays divided?

Friends: Spend time alone with friends, as a couple
              or both?

Meals: Supper at six p.m.? At least one meal
              together each day?

Hobbies: Time and money devoted to each?

Other topics to consider:

1. Television in the bedroom?
2. Bed covers tucked or corners freed?

3. Which way for the bathroom tissue to unroll –top or bottom?
4. Get up when the alarm goes off or hit the snooze button how many times maximum?
5. Squeezing of the toothpaste?
6. Will you save change? If so, who will roll it and take the rolls to the bank? Saving coins for a special purpose?
7. Will you leave at the last possible moment to go somewhere, or will you consistently give yourselves some wiggle room?

Let whoever cares the most win.

Never is a good time for illness, a crisis or an emergency. Talk through hypothetical scenarios.

Know exactly how they prefer their coffee or tea and be willing to prepare it for them if they are sick, running late, need a favor, or as a pleasant surprise. Be prepared for them to melt into your arms.

In marriage, joy is multiplied and sorrow is divided. Prefer one another, be considerate, and be nice – 'til death do you part may be a very long time.

You think you may know what to expect? Being a man and then being a husband is different from being a man. Same for the woman, a wife is different.

Marry young. Stay close to multi-generational help and work in the family business if possible. Childbearing is easier young. Don't wait until you are forty years old to try to start your family.

Let thy fountain be blessed; and rejoice with the wife of your youth…and be thou ravished always with her love (Proverbs 5:18, 19b).

"It is not a lack of love, but a lack of friendship that makes unhappy marriages."

Friedrich Nietzsche

"Marriage is not a noun."

Barbara DeAngelis

"Charity begins at home."

Sir Thomas Browne, 1642

Wherefore they are no more twain, but one flesh. What therefore God hath joined together, let no man put asunder (Proverbs 21:21).

Grandmother's Advice to Ladies on Necessities

1. Lipstick is easy—one for the purse, one for the makeup area, and one in the freezer for good measure.
2. Bras are easy—one to wear, one to wash, and one to rest.
3. Fragrance is easy—cologne spray for every day, perfume for extra pampering, and bath powder as a matter of principle.
4. Do you or your lady buy multiple lipsticks, bras, and fragrances due to the fear of their favorites being discontinued?
5. Ladies, without fail, always wear a good fitting bra, and apply lipstick and fragrance before you step out of the house.

"Be the woman he wakes up for."

Jen Michelle

Grandmother's Advice for Gentlemen

1. Be punctual.
2. Hold doors for ladies, children and the elderly.
3. Always carry a handkerchief in case a lady needs it.
4. Listen with your eyes, too.
5. Dress appropriately for all occasions.
6. Quality over quantity and shine your shoes!
7. When invited to someone's home, bring a gift.
8. Maintain good posture and be impeccably groomed.
9. Be kind and respectful to all.
10. Learn how to build a fire, grill, pack a picnic, and dance.
11. Never kiss and tell.

Grandmother's Advice on Friends

1. They may steal your boyfriend/ girlfriend.
2. They may lie to you.
3. They may disrespect your belongings.

"Knowing when to walk away is wisdom. Being able to is courage. Walking away with grace, and your head held high, is dignity."

Rita Ghatourey

Events may be trying. It is not the actual circumstance that is the real issue. Only you can change your mind and attitude. Dwell on the best/ right outcome and dare to act in that direction.

With perceived slights—it could be a misunderstanding due to less-than-ideal communication. Their perception is their reality. Holding a grudge only hurts you. Be kind. Forgive others, forgive yourself, and move on.

…Love your enemies, do good to them which hate you, bless them that curse you, and pray for them which despitefully use you (Luke 6:27b-28).

Grandmother's Advice on Sleep

Play the still and quiet game. Be as still as possible, notice your breath. Slowly relax your body starting with your toes, being grateful for each and every part. Afterward, count your other blessings and you will fall asleep before you know it.

When thou liest down, thou shalt not be afraid: Yea, thou shalt lie down, and thy sleep shall be sweet (Proverbs 3:24).

I will both lay me down in peace, and sleep: for thou, Lord, only makest me dwell in safety (Psalm 4:8).

This I recall to my mind; therefore have I hope. It is of the LORD's mercies that we are not consumed, because his compassions fail not. They are new every morning: great is thy faithfulness (Lamentations 3:21-23).

Grandmother's Advice on the Solution for Pre-Dread is to Fret Not

Child: Worrying in advance.

Adult: "A man that suffers before it is necessary suffers more than is necessary."

Seneca

Whereas ye know not what shall be on the morrow. For what is your life? It is even a vapor, that appeareth for a little time, and then vanisheth away (James 4:14).

Grandmother's Advice on Control

The sooner you realize you cannot do anything about:

The weather,

The traffic, and

Other people,

The happier you will be.

Grandmother's Advice in a Nutshell

Blessed are the flexible for they shall not be bent out of shape.

Study with a sincere desire to learn.

Beware: Discouragement is the devil's greatest tool.

Being single is to be an unclaimed blessing.

"I've learned that people will forget what you said, people will forget what you did, but people will never forget how you made them feel."

Maya Angelou

"Fulfillment is a longer lasting emotion over happiness."

Robert Greene

What do you do when you see a stern woman with her hands on her hips? RUN!

Learn to say *no* graciously.

Learn to communicate gratitude sincerely.

Learn to realize your dream is only through action daily.

You know you are graduating from senior citizen to elderly when your eyebrows begin to turn white. Maintain a close circle of family, neighbors and friends. Care for them and they will be there for you.

I used to be caustically sarcastic. I overcame this through prayer and by applying Benjamin Franklin's method of consciously working at it every waking hour, engaging in continuous self-improvement to become more civilized.

Hate is an extraordinarily harsh word to be used sparingly. Cruelty, injustice, and the shedding of innocent blood, first come to mind, and then two much less harsh words would be pet peeves:

1. Being accused of something I am not guilty of.

2. Paying for things that are not my fault. Example: Graffiti Removal in playing Monopoly

3. Being rushed or late.

4. A milk mess.

In Ryan Holiday's *The Daily Stoic*, I learned of Marcus Aurelius saying, "Be tolerant with others and strict with yourself." This is my new motto.

However, I am still so competitive I cannot even play putt-putt.

Grandmother's Post Script

Do not chase happiness.

Happiness is a by-product of striving.

Enjoy the diligent pursuit - the adventure,

The achievement,

The accomplishment,

And the success will taste even sweeter.

My prayer is that our children, grandchildren and great-grandchildren would walk upright and with the Lord. I pray for their salvation, health and safety… the good ones and the wayward ones, especially.

Chapter 12
Aging Gracefully

How is it we can remember the music of the 60's and 70's—every single word and can't remember why we went to the refrigerator, into the next room or where our glasses are located? Are you tired of leaving your cell phone on the roof of the car and having a neighbor call and call trying to help you find it?

"If I'd known I'd live this long, I'd have taken better care of myself, especially the upper arms."

"Aging seems to be the only available way to live a long life."
Kitty O'Neill Collins
American stuntwoman and high-speed racer

"Be needy or needed? Be needed. Be of service. It's a happier way to live."
Rabbi Manis Friedman

Bravo

For Valentine's Day, Jim asked me what I needed or wanted.

I said "Grab-bars installed in the master bath."

My hero.

Lost?

Traveling with Jim for work in Indiana,

First night after supper, we parked and I entered a department store.

Recalling a huge blue jean display at the entrance,

Coupon in hand went upstairs to find a bargain.

After twenty minutes of roaming,

Took the escalator down and walked outside.

Jim was nowhere.

His rental car was black and square.

Searched the parking lot and called his cell phone.

Dead – he left it at the apartment to charge.

Hoping he had gone to get the phone,

I called again and left a message to please come back, ready to go.

9:00 p.m. approached.

Back inside, a compassionate sales lady sat me down.

Finally, I had the good sense to ask if there was another entrance.

She said, "Yes, on the north side," and pointed the way.

There another brand's blue jeans were on full display.

Outside, Jim was listening to the radio, patiently waiting.

He was unfazed.

Humiliated, I cried with relief all the way back to the apartment.

Overwhelmed Multi-tasker?
8 a.m.

Dropped Wade off at High School

Drove the shortcut towards home.

Forgot what I was supposed to do next.

Pulled into Academy's parking lot to be still and calm down,

Closed my eyes and stopped to think.

I'm safe, but disconcerted.

Had left my planner on the desk.

Finally, remembered to go to Sam's for gas, and

To pick up produce afterwards.

Solution: Stop multi-tasking. Focus.

Also, type notes in the phone and write on your hand.

There is No Way to Make this Stuff Up
August 20, 2023, Writing at 3:35 a.m.

Yesterday I needed to go to Wellspring to feed the oncidium orchid that has not yet sold. I called Nora to see if she would like to ride along and run a few errands for a little outing. She is due to get a new hip in September. Earlier, she had been out, so she was resting, but was able to come along. Wellspring Treasures closes at 3 o'clock on Saturdays so we needed to get a move on.

As I picked up the orchid to take it to the work room, Jim called and said he had finished his work in Louisville, Kentucky and was headed back to Ft. Wayne, Indiana. I talked to him and continued fooling with the orchid. I had fed the home orchids earlier and brought the remaining food for the oncidium in a Mason jar. After hanging up with Jim, I fed the orchid and grabbed a bottle of water from our refrigerator and my purse, put the orchid back on display in the showroom, and went next door to get Nora to run on to the drugstore and post office. Afterwards, we decided to go to one more store. It was quarter of four after that and we decided to eat supper. Then, I took her home and said I would see her shortly to take care of our foster kittens in her basement. Once home, I went for the phone in my purse to check the weather and it was not there. I looked everywhere and searched the car and found a bag of Nora's we failed to grab earlier. I walked the bag up and told her I had lost the phone again. As I took care of the kittens she called the restaurant where we dined to see if a purple phone with a golden retriever screen saver had been found. As I left her basement, she said she would call me every five minutes to see if I could hear it ringing. Back home, all I heard was the still calm silence.

Long story short, Pat called the stores we visited and she loaned me her son, Isaiah's phone in case I needed to call 911.

Recently I had left the phone in the ladies room at QT in Duncan and most recently on the top of the Prius. I prayed for the Lord to help us find it again.

Later I called Jim and he was not amused. I had promised to keep the phone on the hot pink lanyard he bought. It is handy; however, inconvenient because the side straps are in the way of the buttons so I am not 100% happy with it. We rehashed the day step by step and determined the phone must be at Wellspring because that was where I had forgotten I used it last, talking to him before feeding the oncidiium. I remembered picking up my handbag and grabbing a bottle of water. I must have left the phone on our break table because I also forgot to get the empty Mason jar that had contained the liquid orchid food. At ten o'clock Monday morning, we will know the truth. The phone and the jar have a 99% chance of being on the table waiting.

I remembered Jim saying the lanyard was supposed to fit the phone perfectly so I must have been using it upside down.

Lesson learned: Quit multi-tasking. Focus.

Update: Yes, the phone and Mason jar were where I had left them, and yes I am wearing the phone in the hot pink lanyard right side up. This will save us from having to pay Life Alert for now.

...all things work together for good to them that love the God... (Romans 8:28).

Gracefully Aging

As our family and social circle narrows,

We say goodbye to friends and loved ones due to death and disease.

The constant fear of falling and not being able to get up again haunts most

Bionic Boomers and Super Seniors.

Let's have patience and empathy for all who remain and

Stay flexible to help one another

Navigate the physical and technological challenges ahead.

Most evenings I catch the sunset and

Light the candles on the katio if it is not too hot.

The evening has officially begun.

Most mornings, I am up before the sunrise and

Can catch a glimpse before it rises high and

Disappears into the multi-shaded green canopy.

The day has officially begun.

I hope to see another sunset and another sunrise,

But you never know which one will be your last. One will.

How I want to be remembered:

1. As a prayer warrior

2. As an encourager

3. As a good listener

4. As a good cook

I have fought a good fight, I have finished my course, I have kept the faith... (2 Timothy 4:7a).

If the Creek Doesn't Rise and it Doesn't Snow, We Will Go

If the good Lord lets us live, our next-door neighbor, Nora, will be eighty this Thanksgiving. Her cousin-in-law, Reida, will be ninety in the spring. Being the baby in the bunch, I will be seventy-three this Halloween.

Reida and I were each other's customer in the 1980's. She had a boutique in Inman and I had Sarah Ann's Undercover World in Spartanburg. Nora married Reida's cousin in 1962 and they have remained close friends and enjoyed dining out and shopping together throughout the years.

In recent years, we have gone thrift shopping together starting in Columbus, North Carolina, moving through Tryon, Landrum, and back to Spartanburg if we have not worn each other out yet. Once we take off, there is no telling where we will go, what we will buy or where we will eat. Last trip, we decided upon Side Street Pizza in Tryon for lunch, and my granddaughter, Paulina, was also there. I was glad for this twenty-two-year-old young lady to see three amazing vibrant little old ladies having fun, enjoying their food and being alive… laughing and having a good time like we are all in our twenties.

Each time we go on an adventure across the state line, we are somewhat slower and a little more fragile; however, still spry, mobile enough and forever savvy - thankful to be walking, talking, and in our right minds. It has been a blessing to be with the two remarkable confident ladies – to hear their banter and soak up their wisdom.

Rebuke not an elder, but intreat...the elder women as mothers; the younger as sisters... (Timothy 5:1-2).

Minimalist to the Very End

If you can't bring me flowers while I am living,

I sure don't want them when I am dead.

Just visit the memorial garden in Richland County

For I have donated my body to MUSC.

It is the least expensive way to go to medical school.

Final note:

If you have made it to this point, I am eternally grateful. My hope and prayer is that if this has helped even just one person to have more joy or to be encouraged, my mission has been accomplished, and all the glory is given to our Father in heaven above.

Thank you.

Recommended Reading

1. The Bible – Shows us the way to live, avoid unnecessary suffering, and has the right answer to every question.

2. All of Og Mandino

3. All of Dr. Kirk H. Neely

4. Man's Search for Meaning, Viktor Frankl

5. How to Win Friends and Influence People, Dale Carnegie

6. The One Minute Manager, K. Blanchard PhD and S. Johnson, MD

7. The Gentle Art of Swedish Death Cleaning, Margareta Magnusson

8. The More of Less, Joshua Becker

9. The Autobiography of Benjamin Franklin, Ben Franklin

10. The Power of Positive Thinking, Norman Vincent Peale

Preview of Upcoming Book

Fifteen Pounds of Love Letters with a Ton of Hope

After clearing our Mother's house after she passed away, Jim and I took her antique cedar chest home and placed it at the foot of our bed. The chest proved to be quite in the way; however, convenient for putting on our shoes. I called my brother, Doug and asked if he and Laury would enjoy the chest in their Virginia home. They said *yes,* and in the spring of 2021, we delivered the cedar chest.

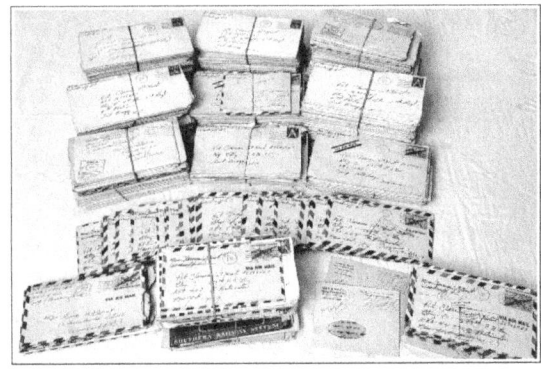

The chest contained some of Doug's baby clothes, his report cards, Bible School crafts and fifteen pounds of love letters. Mother and Daddy wrote these before and during WWII and they contained a ton of hope for their future after the war.

Our Christian parents were not perfect, but close enough. We hope to be able to present their story in a reverent manner because the letters were private, in their own handwriting, and meant only for one another; however, a true-love story needs to be shared and we will make every effort to do our best.

About the Author

Photo by Kate Wiggins 8/30/23

Native of Spartanburg, South Carolina, Karen WeHunt Harden graduated from Limestone College. After public accounting and retail careers, she graduated from Culinary School in the Spartanburg/Greenville Technical College system. Since retiring from Foodservice, Karen volunteers at Wellspring Treasures and Habitat for Humanity. Her Upcycled4Charity venture benefits Habitat, Hatcher Garden, and *Speak for Animals* auctions. She and her brother, Doug, published *A Five and Dime's Million-Dollar Baby* in August, 2023.

Karen is a Downsizing/ Minimalist Coach, animal lover, and enjoys her orchids, writing, and grand-parenting with Jim, her beloved husband of thirty-eight years.

Made in the USA
Columbia, SC
29 December 2023

29622534R00068